Without Blossoms

Jenna Tung

BookLeaf
Publishing

India | USA | UK

Dedication

To those who feel bare, yet remain whole

Acknowledgements

All my love and thanks goes to my friends:

Andrea Patton

who encouraged me, helped edit this book, and got drunk and read poetry with me on multiple occasions. The world best believe Andi can drink seven shots, and she can write a damn good poem about it.

Elena Franklin

who cured my writers block, tries to cure me, inspired some of these words, and wrote with me the songs I turned into poems.

1. Chinatown

I was blowing bubbles in Chinatown,
a fresh runaway
who thought of nothing.

I was smoking out the window of a cab.
I thought about cancer.
I thought about dying.

I was tossing pennies into a wishing well.
They hit the bottom—
the dark, rock bottom.

I swam down until I reached the dark, rock bottom,
where I became some bottom-feeding microbial form of
life,
unable to thrive,
sucking up
all the bad medication,
all the bad luck.

Finally, I was nothing more than a drugged-up animal
in San Francisco,
where all the windows waited for:
bubbles,

smoking,
jumping,
dying.

But when I was blowing bubbles in Chinatown,
I thought about nothing
not even myself.

2. Ohayō

Reading *Snow Country,*
Starving for romance.

When the sun came out today in Kyoto,
I wanted to tell you
when will you make me feel like the sun did?

3. How deeply the fields

How deeply the fields
are empty all afternoon,
with wine-colored grass.

Oh, my favorite song.

4. Vampire

What if I'd rather meet death by burning?
What if I don't need the sun where I'm going?

I'll miss seeing it on your bare skin
and homemade breakfast in the sun-swallowed kitchen.

Now you're waking up.
You'd get a lot more done
if you didn't marry me.

I won't be like my mom
if I don't want to be like her.
But how can you be sure?

5. The Jam and The Jelly

Corey from *Empire Records* said,
"You won't be like your mother if you don't want to be
like her."

Still, somehow you wind up with a freezer full of berries
you picked yourself,
Drink like a fish with seasonal depression,
and all the love you create spoils slowly,
like the jam and jelly in somebody else's refrigerator.

You also cry for a long time alone in a pretty town,
slurring that the sun makes you feel better than anything
else,
and you forget it all by tomorrow, just as planned.

There's that little part of a daughter that's angry, feels
diseased,
who drunk drives home to her family.
There's that sickening feeling when she crashes into
someone else's.

And your sleepy, steady breathing is making me feel
really fucking lonely,
like you're gonna leave me.

We wake up, our mouths taste funny,
until they taste the same.
The sun hits your face,
makes me promise I won't be jaded today,
allows that little part of me some acceptance.

6. Nothing tastes

Nothing tastes.
Every naked picture a mistake,
and happiness a mystery.

Nothing that you feel is that unique.
I count your words like pills.
When they're gone, I can't say anything.

Nothing can stop me from hiding your car keys
in case you leave me.
When they're gone, I don't have anything.

Now you're coming up the drive,
you couldn't find
any sign of life
beyond our property line.

Nothing tastes
as good as my dependence.

7. Pieces of Moon

She gives to you
pieces of the moon,
as stars fall from your eyes.
Beneath your blindfold,
you carry two swords
over your heart, if a heart was a swollen ice cube.

She gives to you
ingenious tools,
writes stories too, and
shares them with you first.
She cheats on men
and can climb anything there is to latch onto.

Too smart to take birth control
or have children with beasts.
She misses you.
Psychic love is far beyond
the progress of psychiatry.
Synchronicities,
your conspiracies
and theories, she turns into philosophy,
giving you more and more
pieces of the moon.

8. Like a Branch Without Blossoms

Eye level with the mattress you laid on, a shack floor.
We'd crawl through the window and lay together on the
roof all night,
like dead stars on the boulevard,
like bugs in the wintertime.
Remember when you said
you wouldn't be too surprised if someday I go missing?

Like a branch without blossoms, I'm not worth seeing
now.

So look down.
Now look up.
Catch your eye on a prettier planet you think has yet to
be discovered.

Like a branch without blossoms,
a sky without stars,
a chicken without a head,
a cadaver without molars,
a washed-up rockstar,
an unknown soap star,
a world without muscles that work or cars,

abandonment-guilt-filled mothers,
an ending to a movie you just saw.

I knew how things would turn out,
and like a branch without blossoms,
is it not worth looking back on?

9. Wings on tar

You found a soft spot,
I've got a new cut.
When I'm so used to waking up
with nothing moving in my heart,
an emptiness
that you fill for Jesus.
When I'm so used to waking up with no sunlight in my
heart.

But now, so in love,
I can't see,
and you
an oncoming vehicle.
I'll let you gently peel my wings up off the tar.

Yeah, if you'll be a good liar,
I'll be a good dog guarding the front door,
hardly able to wait
to lick your criminal face.

10. Uncanny Valley

I don't believe in you anymore,
or the causes for war.
What a contradiction,
when all signs of life make me nauseous.

Though that's all I ever wanted—
life, to make me nauseous
in the mornings as our baby grew in my belly.

But Earth
is the uncanny valley,
according to space exploration,
infested with uncanny beings
who write love letters
and sign them sincerely,
which helps create more uncanny beings.

The endangered species lurks pragmatically,
but is often fooled and fondled by the uncanny
who love pragmatic beings.
They watch them on TVs
that eat their brains,
but it's a necessity
that they learn to imitate

in order to enter their honeymoon phase.

I take my shots,
I shoot you straight—
Honest Abe,
trigger-happy.
A spade is not a fucking ace.
No, not even bullets can open your mind.

11. I want to live again

15

I know this before I take my morning medication.
I know this because I almost forget to take it in the
afternoon.

But I can't remember a damn thing.
Not the names of the neighbors who say hello when I'm
gardening,
or of the flowers I plant, cut, and put into vases—
the ones I quietly set on porches of those who entertain
my existence.

I love living,
or else I'm amazing at pretending,
and if that's all it takes,
I'm living a movie

12. My reintroduction to death

From death, I conjured her —
the reincarnation of Sylvia Plath moved in next door.

With my 30th year almost killing me,
or me almost killing my 30th year,
she says she understands.
Now that I'm an actual negative of a photograph,
my friend, the reincarnation of Sylvia Plath,
she reintroduced me to death.

I take her words with me as I walk home,
and using them, write my very own
death poems.

When I told her about this,
she said, "My poems about death are not published."
I was surprised to hear,
and I realized I had made a mistake by wishing her here
—

all of her poems about death were real.

But now she knows the modernity of murder.

Trash is literally filling the earth,
and the post-feminism movements feel oddly familiar.

17

13. Pink Rose, Blue Bottle

A pink rose stands in a blue glass bottle,
once filled with alcohol,
label torn off.

So blue.
I painted flowers that cried
on the canvas I had saved for a masterpiece
that would never be
because I wasn't good at art,
I was good at drinking.

And staying up for two days,
creating mistake after mistake,
until they turned into something
somewhat beautiful.
Something that made me want to look away
forever, sometimes.

14. Wedding Present

I am not bulletproof.
I am stained
even more so with each day
I've spent looking out from this porch,
waiting for new admirers.

15. Barfly

She's a barfly
if something's on her mind, she'll tell you.
Polyamorous
most of the time.
We fly down I-65,
in the same clothes we wore last night.
She's singing my new favorite song,
and she's not afraid of dying.

She's chaotic
like the time she drove to Memphis
and framed a man.
Her only real commitment
is her drug addiction—
steady as the sunrise,
pulling her back every morning.

She's science fiction
but I've seen her cry
listening to a song about losing faith.
I listen to her dreams of electric sheep,
her false memories,
she just wants to believe.

—————-

Does it make you wish you were a better person?

It can make you sick
Wanting what you're missing
there's plenty of fish
in the ocean
you can have your pick
but you wanted that one

You'll solve your problems by laying on the roof for
awhile
and if this baby is mine, my best friend will drive

And now you want to be who I thought you were?
have all the stars finally lost their wonder?

you had everything

now you're slobbering
because I'm disappearing
out of mind
dying
like the ocean
and your belly's aching?

my belly's aching
you look primitive

it makes me want to have a daughter and tell her she's
beautiful
and that she's everything

16. Cowgirl

I don't know who I am yet
Thought about it on the road for a while.
Mama, when you were a cowgirl,
did it hurt to change your mind?

And did you cry because it was your fault?
Should I just drive or take another shot?
What if I die, nobody at all?

I don't know, but I crashed it.
I guess I'll drink a little less for a while.
Mama, when you were a cowgirl,
did you have to pay some fines?

And did you cry because it was your fault?
Should I just ride or marry a big shot?
Tell me why this shame feels natural.
What if I die, nobody at all?

And I know I was blind,
all of the women.
Mama, when you were a cowgirl,
did you ignore the same signs?

And did you cry because it wasn't your fault?
Should I just ride and bury this big shot?
And if I don't make the big time,
will I die living a lie?

17. Out of mind, dying like the ocean

Does it make you wish you were a better person?

It can make you sick,
wanting what you're missing.
There's plenty of fish
in the ocean
you can have your pick,
but you wanted that one.

You'll solve your problems by lying on the roof for a
while,
and if this baby is mine, my best friend will drive.

And now you want to be who I thought you were?
Have all the stars finally lost their wonder?

You had everything,
now you're slobbering,
because I'm disappearing
out of mind,
dying like the ocean.
And your belly's aching?
My belly's aching.

You look primitive.
It makes me want to have a daughter
and tell her she's beautiful,
and that she's everything.

18. Dog eat dog

I'll be better off without you
Turned into drinking in the shower,
drinking until I could lie to myself.
It's just a fucking toothbrush,
I could throw out,
but when I look in the mirror,
I can't see a single thing you saw inside.

I got lost in you,
needed you like air.
It started feeling like doing cheap drugs—
you just wanted to chew on my smile,
and I didn't want to come down.

And now I don't want to go to my favorite bars
anymore,
and there's no one to pull over so I can pick flowers from
the side of the road.

I had real love,
and I slaughtered it.
But it's dog eat dog
until I'm all alone,
sucking on your bones.

19. Killer

Trapped in your car in the summer,
a fly,
or that girl who cuts through backyards,
killing flower beds
to be where you are.

Baking on a flagstone,
a worm,
or the girl who cuts up your favorite jacket
and kills your lovers.

20. Pet cat

I cried after sex.
He pet me like a cat wearing a black kimono.
We both wanted to knock my eyes out of my head
I get so fucking sad,
and my phones always dead

21. Die in it

ill show you where it hurts everywhere
like chasing after a best friend
flipping over the handlebars

we're both used to being let down hard
both are parents drank too much
it feels good to talk about that stuff
after years of not feeling good enough

so if it feels good,
die in it
sink into it
like a good Korean drama
or a sad song
If you don't mind leaving the car on